DISCOVERING METALS

Carmel Reilly

Nelson CENGAGE Learning

Australia • Brazil • Japan • Korea • Mexico • Singapore • Spain • United Kingdom • United States

Discovering Metals

Fast Forward
Silver Level 23

Text: Carmel Reilly
Editor: Johanna Rohan
Design: James Lowe
Series design: James Lowe
Production controller: Seona Galbally
Photo research: Michel Cottrill, Gilllian Cardinal
Audio recordings: Juliet Hill, Picture Start
Spoken by: Matthew King and Abbe Holmes
Reprint: Siew Han Ong

Acknowledgements
The author and publisher would like to acknowledge permission to reproduce material from the following sources: Photographs by AAA Collection/ Ronald Sheridan, p 21 right; AKG Images, front cover bottom, pp 1 bottom, 19 right/ Erich Lessing, pp 4, 20; Corbis/ Albrecht G Schaefer, p 5/ Angelo Hornak, p 8 bottom/ Jonathan Blair, p 16; Fotolia/Elvira Schäfer, p 6 left/ Steffen Foerster, p 6 right/ Thomas Brostrom, p 23 bottom right; Getty Images/ National Geographic, p 17; Masterfile/Peter Griffith, p 23 left; PhotoDisc, front cover (background), p 13; Photolibrary/ Dinodia, front cover top, pp 1 top, 10 left/ Joyce Productions, p. 9 left/ JTB Photo, p 9 right/ Photo Researchers, p 12/ Sheila Terry, p 11/ Sinclair Stammers, p 18/ SPL/Kaj Svensson, p 8 top/ The Bridgeman Art Library, back cover, pp. 7 left, 7 right, 14 top, 22; The Art Archive/Historiska Museet Stockholm/ Dagli Orti, p 21 left/ Ironbridge Gorge Museum, p 23 top right/ Musee Cernuschi Paris/Dagli Orti, p 14 bottom/ Museo Civico Udine/Dagli Orti (A), p 15 left/ Museo Nazionale d'Arte Orientale Rome /Dagli Orti, p 10 right/ Prehistoric Museum Moesgard Hojbjerg Denmark/Dagli Orti, pp 3, 15 right, 19 left.

Text © 2007 Cengage Learning Australia Pty Limited
Illustrations © 2007 Cengage Learning Australia Pty Limited

Copyright Notice
This Work is copyright. No part of this Work may be reproduced, stored in a retrieval system, or transmitted in any form or by any means without prior written permission of the Publisher. Except as permitted under the Copyright Act 1968, for example any fair dealing for the purposes of private study, research, criticism or review, subject to certain limitations. These limitations include: Restricting the copying to a maximum of one chapter or 10% of this book, whichever is greater; Providing an appropriate notice and warning with the copies of the Work disseminated; Taking all reasonable steps to limit access to these copies to people authorised to receive these copies; Ensuring you hold the appropriate Licences issued by the Copyright Agency Limited ("CAL"), supply a remuneration notice to CAL and pay any required fees.

ISBN 978 0 17 012701 1
ISBN 978 0 17 012693 9 (set)

Cengage Learning Australia
Level 7, 80 Dorcas Street
South Melbourne, Victoria Australia 3205
Phone: 1300 790 853

Cengage Learning New Zealand
Unit 4B Rosedale Office Park
331 Rosedale Road, Albany, North Shore NZ 0632
Phone: 0508 635 766

For learning solutions, visit cengage.com.au

Printed in China by 1010 Printing International Ltd
6 7 8 15

Evaluated in independent research by staff from the Department of Language, Literacy and Arts Education at the University of Melbourne.

DISCOVERING METALS

Carmel Reilly

Contents

Chapter 1	**The End of the Stone Age**	4
Chapter 2	**Discovering Metals**	6
Chapter 3	**Working Metals**	10
Chapter 4	**Bronze**	12
Chapter 5	**The Bronze Age**	14
Chapter 6	**The Iron Age**	18
Chapter 7	**A Changing World**	20
Glossary and Index		24

Chapter 1

THE END OF THE STONE AGE

The Stone Age is the name given to an early period in history when people made their tools and weapons out of stone.

The Stone Age started more than one million years ago. It finished when people began to replace their stone tools and weapons with those made out of metal.

a weapon made of copper and bone

The Stone Age didn't finish around the world
at the same time.
For example, in places like the Middle East,
it ended about 6000 years ago
when people there started using copper.

people in Papua New Guinea

In other places, like Papua New Guinea,
the Stone Age only ended quite recently,
because the people of that country
didn't discover metal (or know how to use it)
until they had contact with Westerners.

Chapter 2

DISCOVERING METALS

Gold

Gold was probably the first metal to be discovered by humans. It is believed that gold was first used about 8000 years ago.

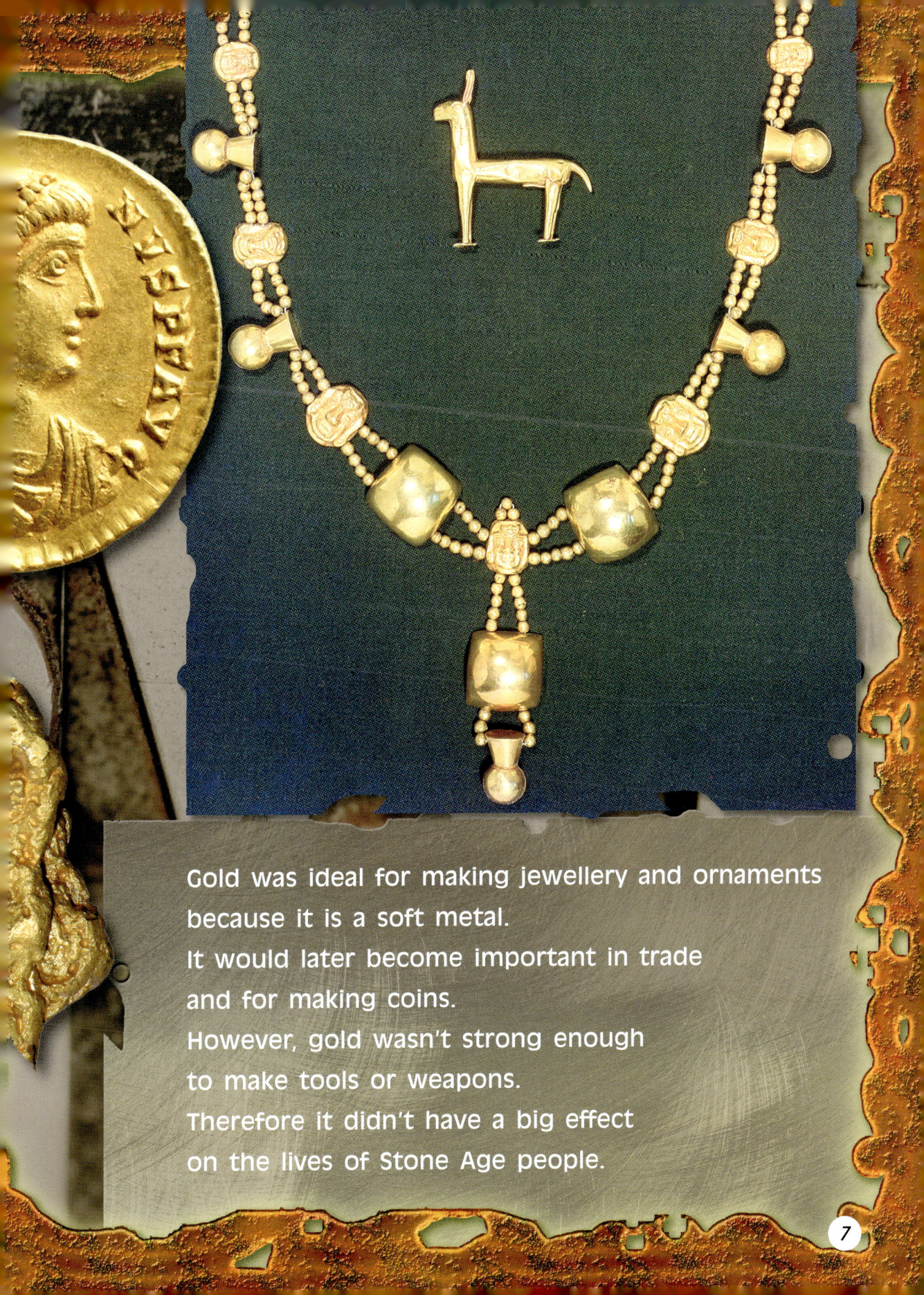

Gold was ideal for making jewellery and ornaments because it is a soft metal.
It would later become important in trade and for making coins.
However, gold wasn't strong enough to make tools or weapons.
Therefore it didn't have a big effect on the lives of Stone Age people.

Copper

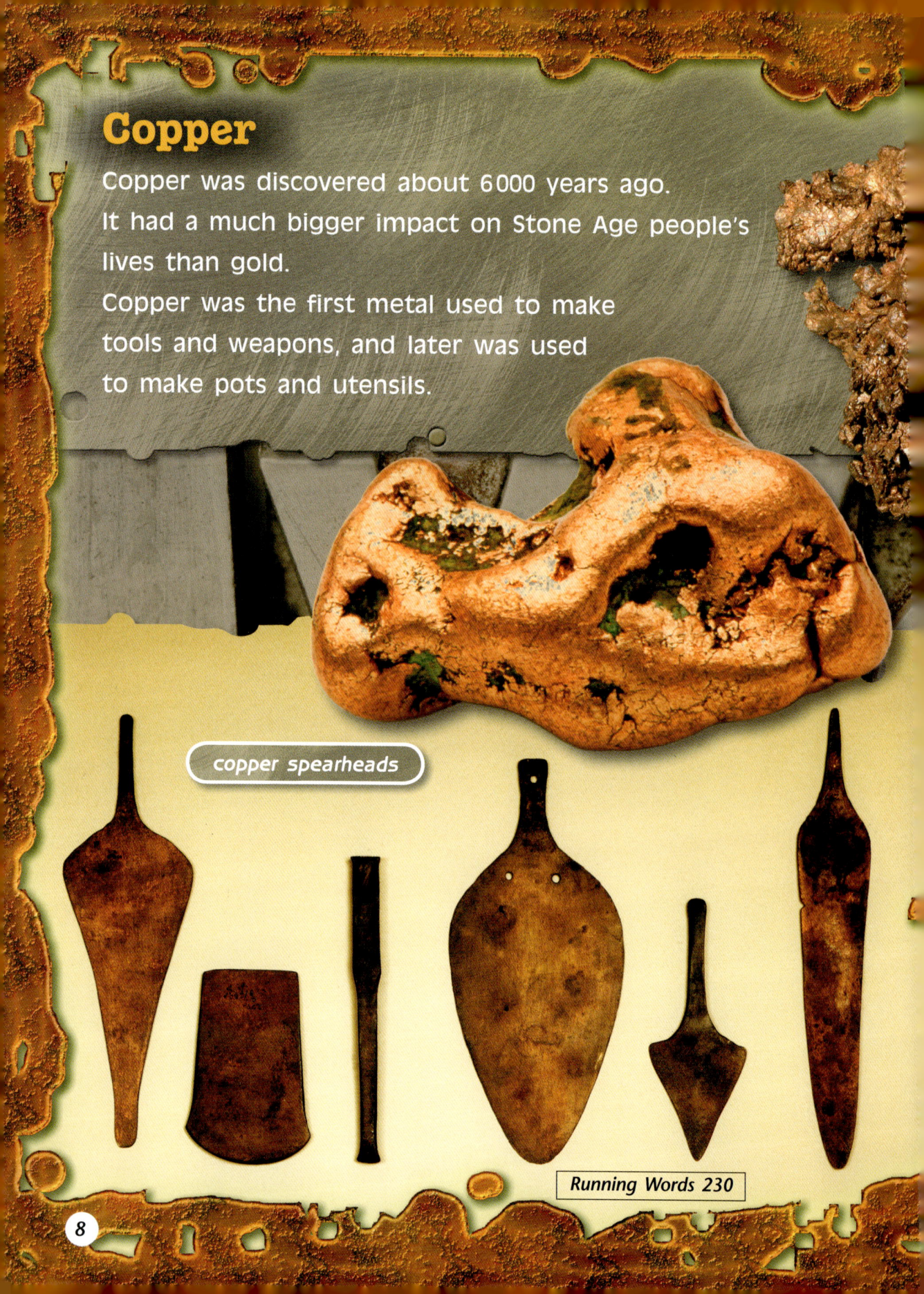

Copper was discovered about 6000 years ago. It had a much bigger impact on Stone Age people's lives than gold.

Copper was the first metal used to make tools and weapons, and later was used to make pots and utensils.

copper spearheads

Running Words 230

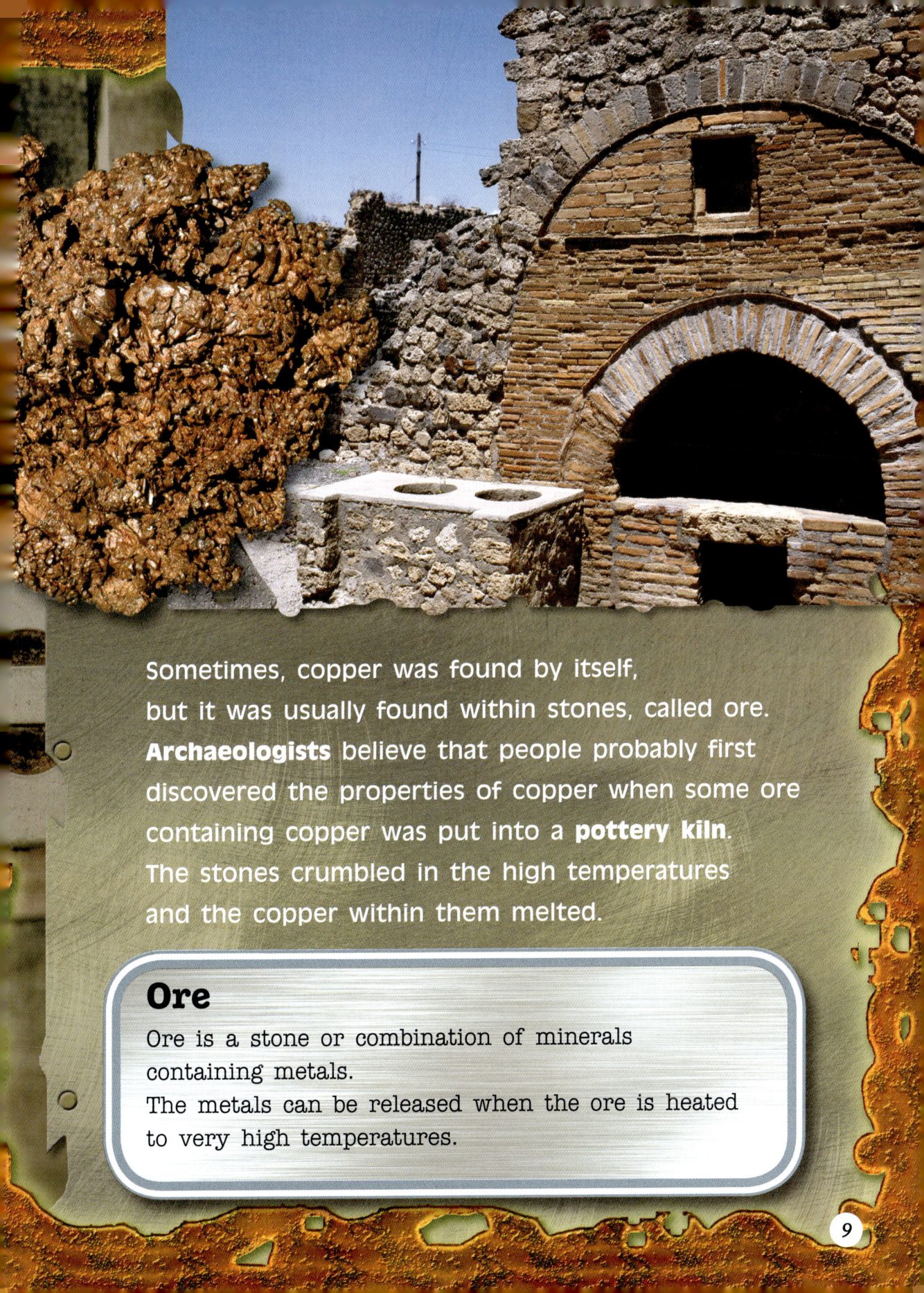

Sometimes, copper was found by itself, but it was usually found within stones, called ore. **Archaeologists** believe that people probably first discovered the properties of copper when some ore containing copper was put into a **pottery kiln**. The stones crumbled in the high temperatures and the copper within them melted.

Ore

Ore is a stone or combination of minerals containing metals.
The metals can be released when the ore is heated to very high temperatures.

Chapter 3

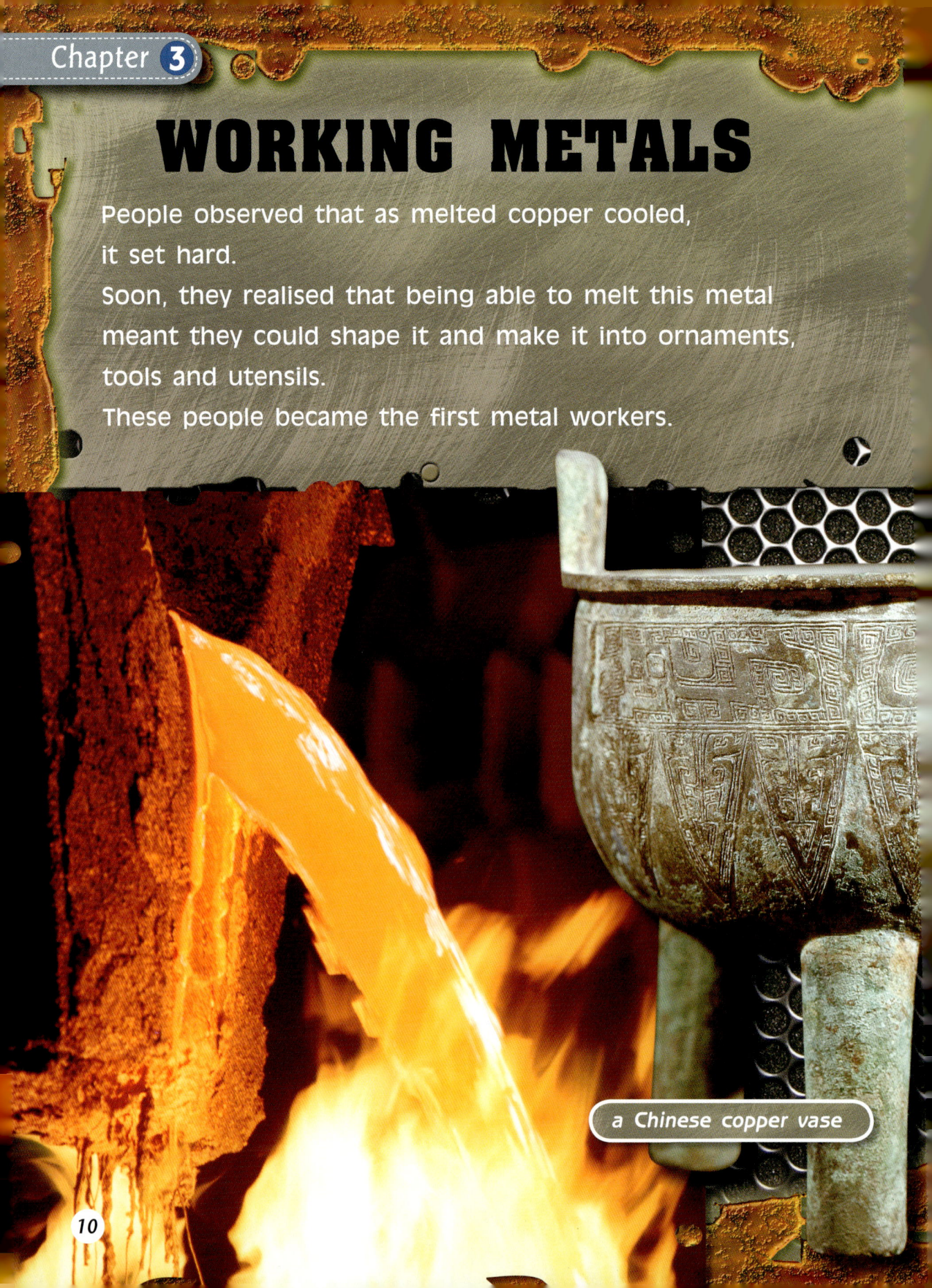

WORKING METALS

People observed that as melted copper cooled, it set hard.

Soon, they realised that being able to melt this metal meant they could shape it and make it into ornaments, tools and utensils.

These people became the first metal workers.

a Chinese copper vase

間吹銅
銀氣を含まざる
あらかねを鑢化し
滓を去りみこれを
間吹銅とらふ

Metal workers worked out how to smelt metal – that is, how to melt ore in order to produce metal from it.
Later, they worked out how to make moulds for the metal so that they could create the exact shapes they wanted.

Chapter 4

BRONZE

In places like China, the Middle East and parts of Europe, another metal – tin – was found near copper.

tin

Metal workers in these places discovered that if tin and copper were mixed together, they became much harder when they set. This new metal was called bronze.

bronze

Alloy

An alloy is a mixture of two or more metals. Metals can be mixed together to give them special properties, such as strength, lightness or flexibility.

Chapter 5

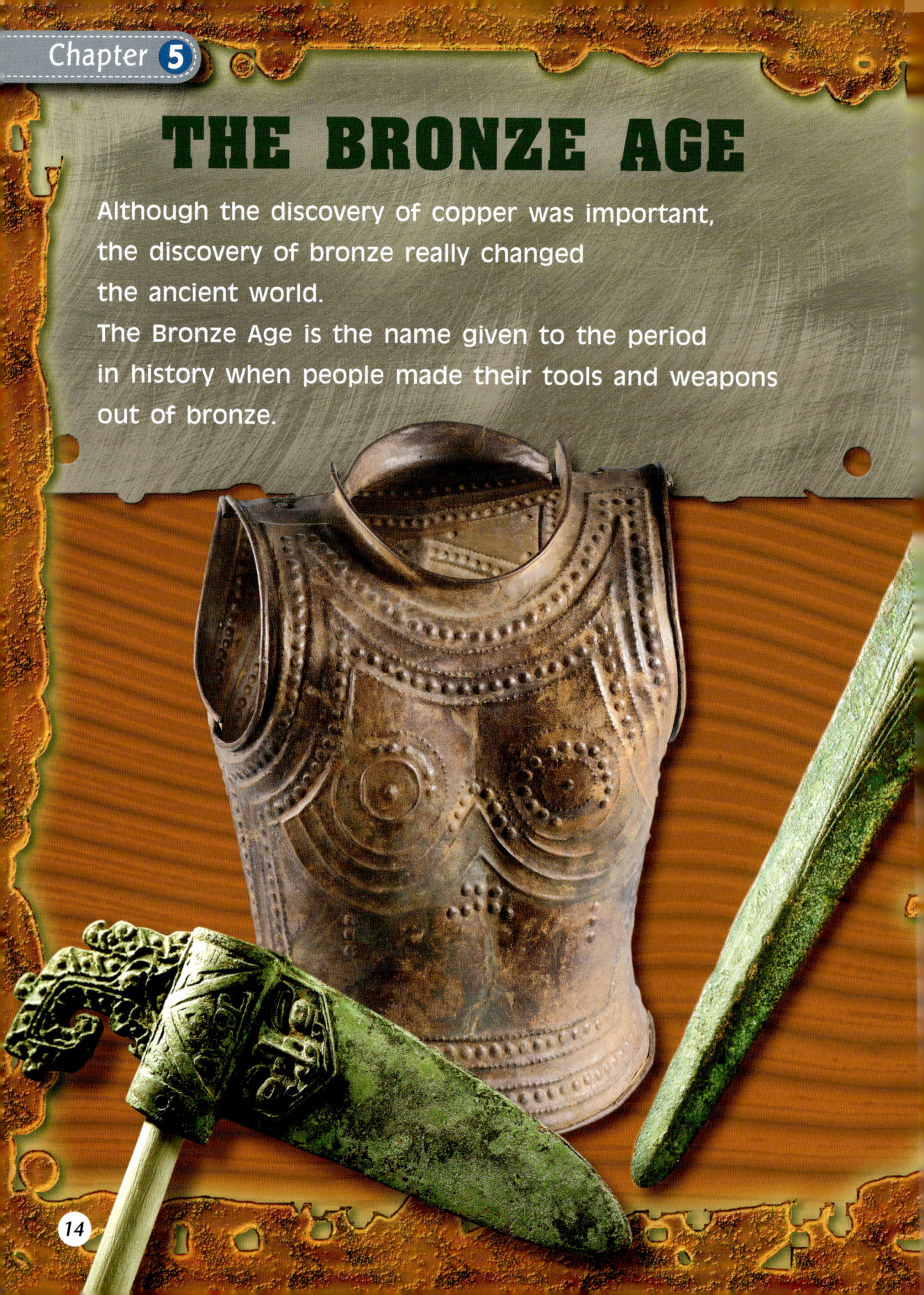

THE BRONZE AGE

Although the discovery of copper was important, the discovery of bronze really changed the ancient world.
The Bronze Age is the name given to the period in history when people made their tools and weapons out of bronze.

Tools made from bronze were harder
and more **durable** than tools made from copper,
and they could be kept sharp more easily.
People could work more quickly
using tools made from bronze.

Better weapons were made from bronze,
such as knives, spears and arrow heads.
This made hunting easier.
Communities who had weapons made from bronze
had an advantage in war
over communities that didn't have them.

A Prized Product

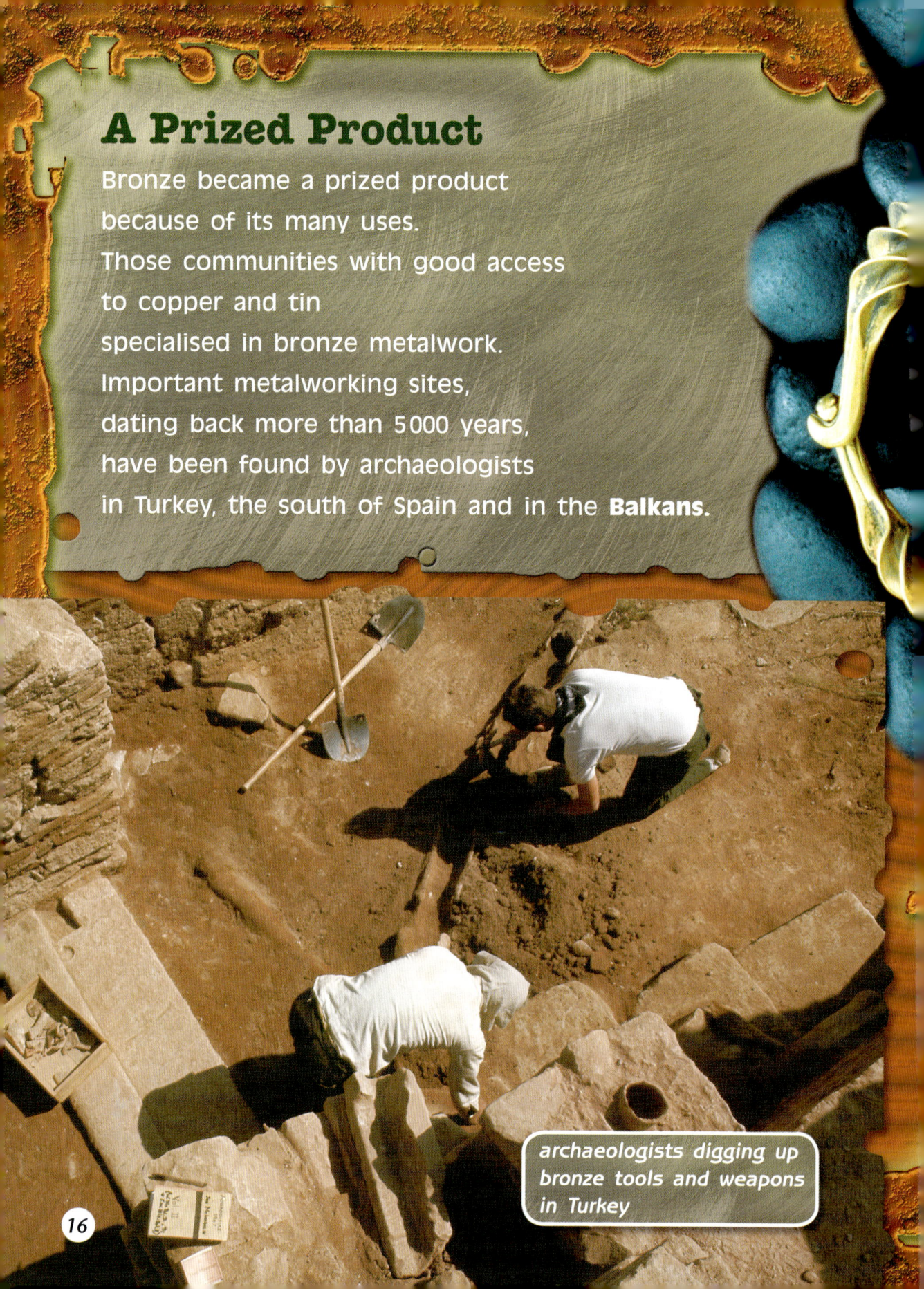

Bronze became a prized product because of its many uses. Those communities with good access to copper and tin specialised in bronze metalwork. Important metalworking sites, dating back more than 5000 years, have been found by archaeologists in Turkey, the south of Spain and in the **Balkans.**

archaeologists digging up bronze tools and weapons in Turkey

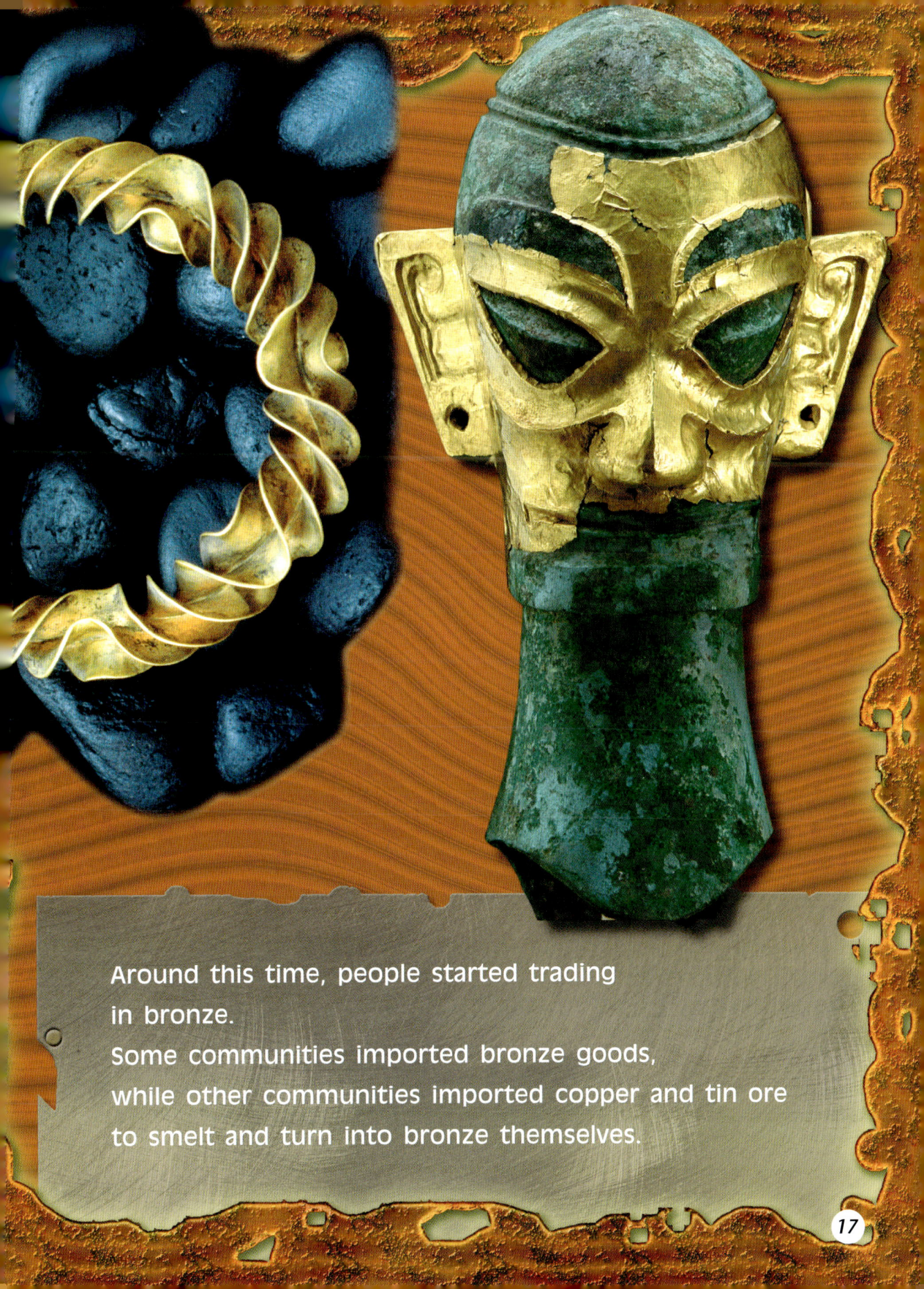

Around this time, people started trading in bronze.
Some communities imported bronze goods, while other communities imported copper and tin ore to smelt and turn into bronze themselves.

Chapter 6

THE IRON AGE

Iron was first used about 3500 years ago. The Iron Age is the name given to the period in history when people made their tools and weapons out of iron.

Although iron ore was common, people took longer to discover its uses because it was harder to smelt than gold, copper and tin. The temperature for melting iron was much higher than for these metals, and special conditions were needed to melt iron.

iron ore

Melting Points of Metals

Tin	232°C
Gold	1062°C
Copper	1084°C
Iron	1535°C

Viking swords made from iron

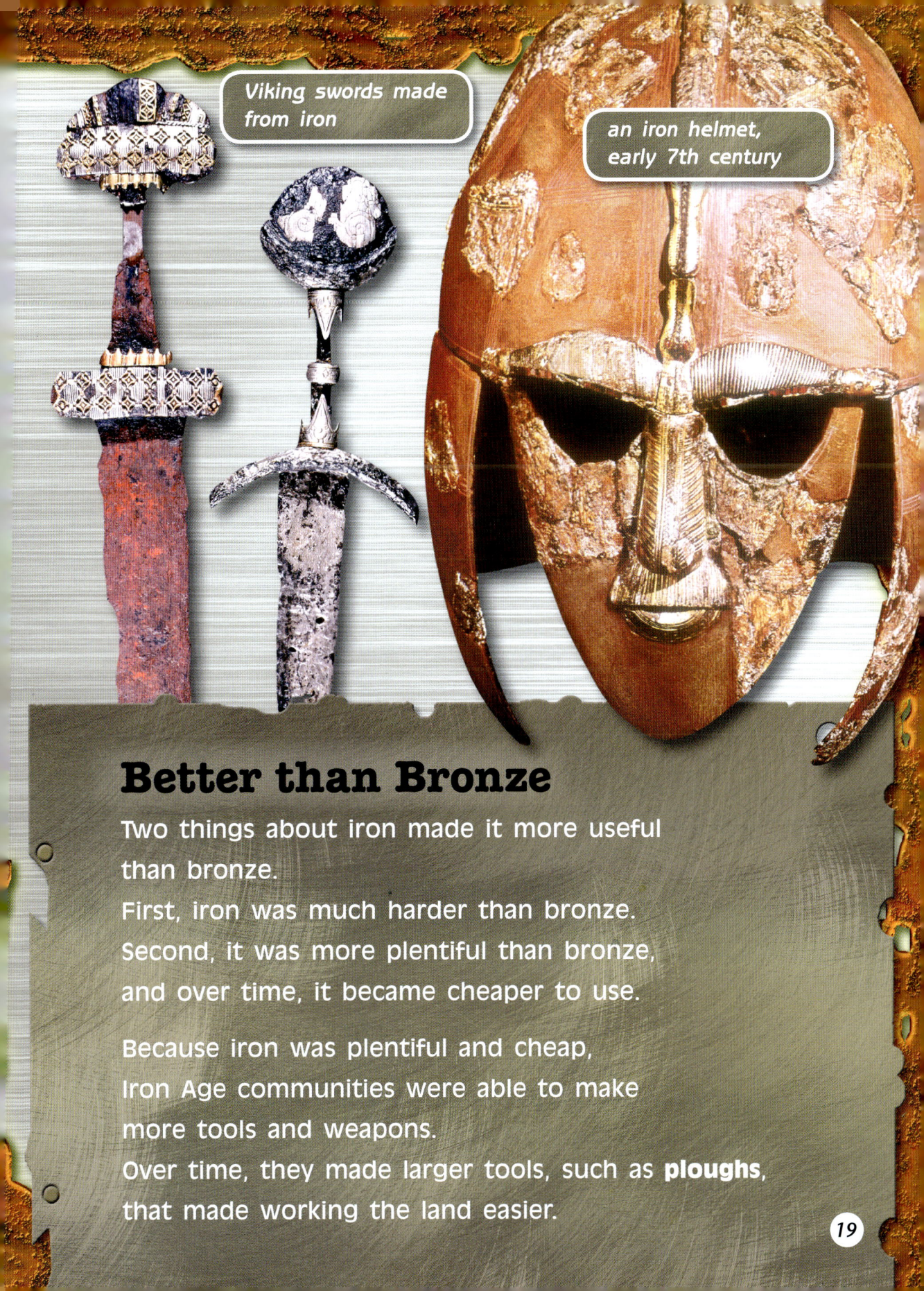

an iron helmet, early 7th century

Better than Bronze

Two things about iron made it more useful than bronze.
First, iron was much harder than bronze. Second, it was more plentiful than bronze, and over time, it became cheaper to use.

Because iron was plentiful and cheap, Iron Age communities were able to make more tools and weapons.
Over time, they made larger tools, such as **ploughs**, that made working the land easier.

Chapter 7

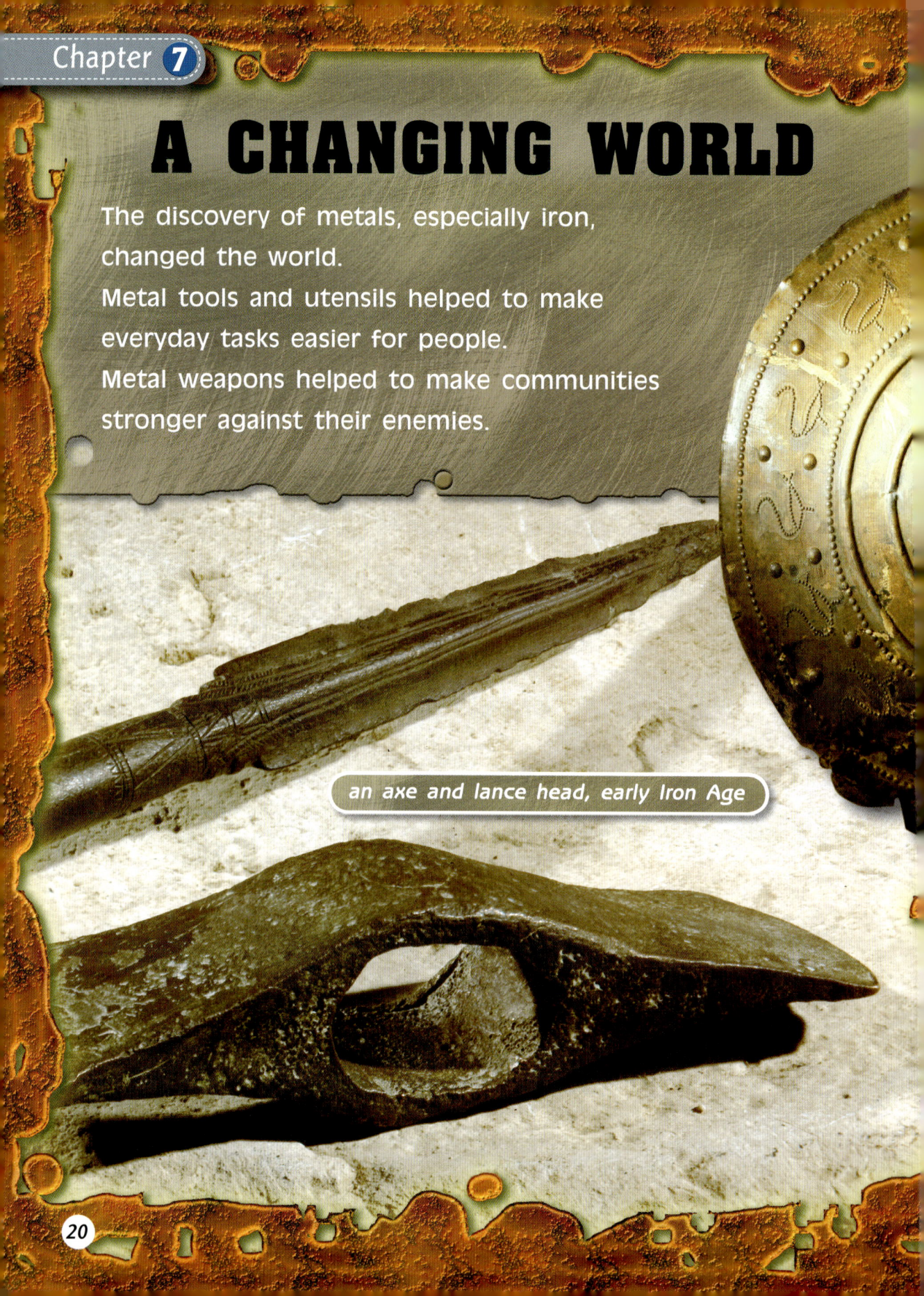

A CHANGING WORLD

The discovery of metals, especially iron, changed the world.

Metal tools and utensils helped to make everyday tasks easier for people.

Metal weapons helped to make communities stronger against their enemies.

an axe and lance head, early Iron Age

a bronze shield, Bronze Age

electrum coins, from Lydia, 600 BC

About 4000 years ago, metal coins were developed. People realised that coins were a good way of exchanging goods and paying people for work they had done.

The use of coins also helped the development of trade and communication between different communities.

Metalworking remained the same for thousands of years. Methods of smelting and **casting** metals didn't change much from the Iron Age until the 1700s. Then, with the coming of the **Industrial Revolution**, metal began to play a bigger role in building and in new technology.

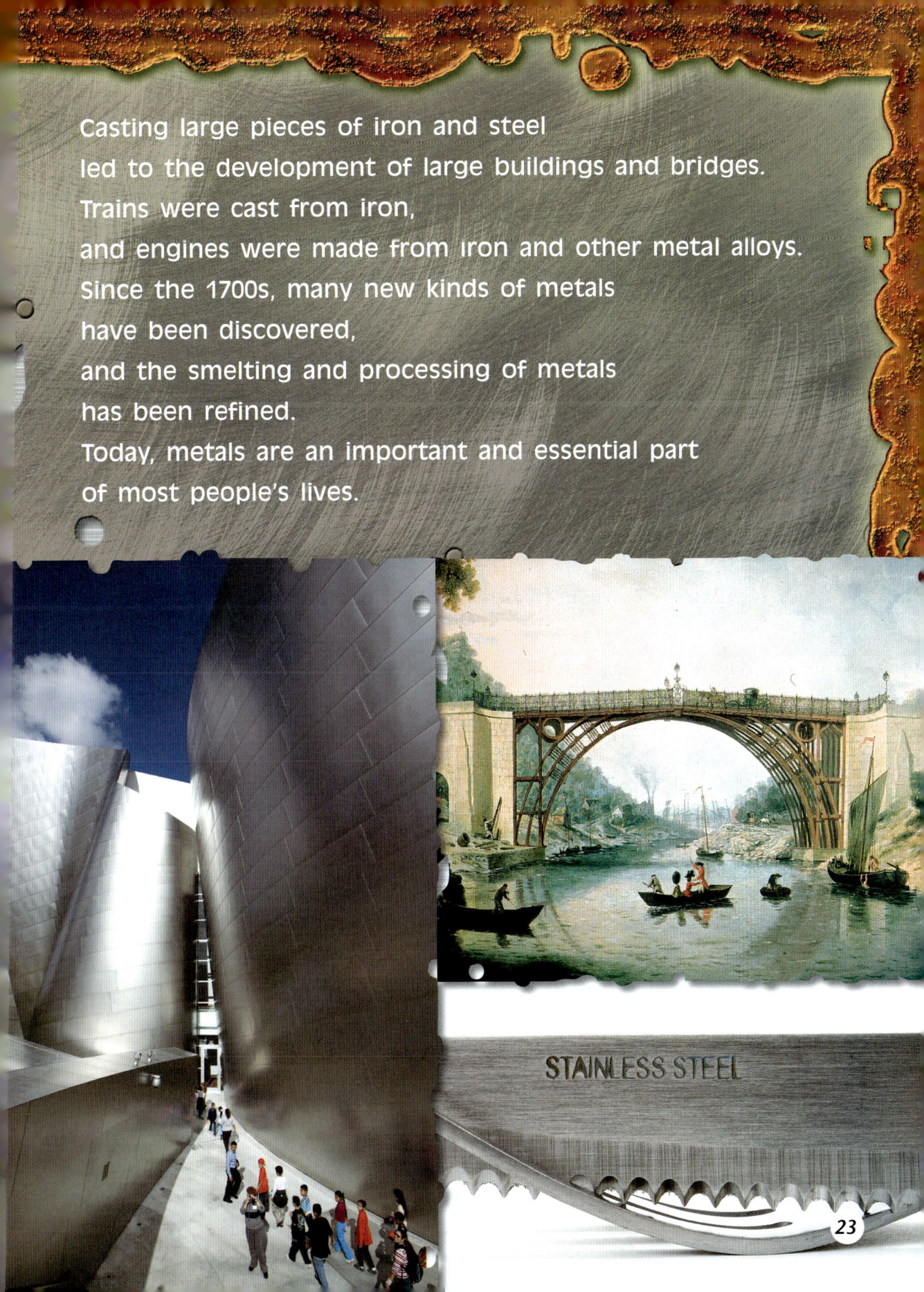

Casting large pieces of iron and steel
led to the development of large buildings and bridges.
Trains were cast from iron,
and engines were made from iron and other metal alloys.
Since the 1700s, many new kinds of metals
have been discovered,
and the smelting and processing of metals
has been refined.
Today, metals are an important and essential part
of most people's lives.

Glossary

archaeologists — people who study history through the recovery and analysis of remains and environmental data

the Balkans — a group of countries in south-eastern Europe

casting — shaping metals by pouring them into a mould

durable — hard-wearing

electrum — a naturally occuring alloy of gold and silver with small amounts of copper

Industrial Revolution — a time (in the late 18th and early 19th centuries) when manual labour was largely replaced by industry and machinery

ploughs — tools used in farming for the cultivation of soil in preparation for planting crops. Ploughs were pulled by humans, oxen or horses.

pottery kiln — a chamber, like an oven, used to fire and harden clay

Index

the Balkans 16
bronze 12–13, 14, 15, 16, 17, 19
China 12
copper 8–9, 10, 12, 13, 15, 16, 18
Europe 12
gold 6–7, 18
iron 18, 19, 20, 23

the Middle East 5, 12
ore 9, 11, 18
Papua New Guinea 5
ploughs 19
steel 23
Stone Age 4, 5, 7, 8
tin 12, 13, 16, 18